EXPLORING OUR SENSES

Hearing

For a free color catalog describing Gareth Stevens' list of high-quality books,
call 1-800-542-2595 (USA) or 1-800-461-9120 (Canada).
Gareth Stevens' Fax: (414) 225-0377.

Library of Congress Cataloging-in-Publication Data

Pluckrose, Henry Arthur.
    Hearing/by Henry Pluckrose; photographs by Chris Fairclough.
        p. cm. -- (Exploring our senses)
    Includes bibliographical references and index.
    Summary: Photographs and text describe loud and soft sounds
heard indoors and outside, made by animals, people, machinery,
and nature.
    ISBN 0-8368-1287-5
    1. Hearing--Juvenile literature. [1. Hearing. 2. Senses and
sensation.] I. Fairclough, Chris, ill. II. Title. III. Series.
QP462.2.P57   1995
612.8'5--dc20   94-23769

North American edition first published in 1995 by
Gareth Stevens Publishing
1555 North RiverCenter Drive, Suite 201
Milwaukee, Wisconsin 53212, USA

This edition © 1995 by Gareth Stevens, Inc. Original edition published in 1985
by The Watts Publishing Group. © 1985 by Watts Books. Additional end matter
© 1995 by Gareth Stevens, Inc.

Additional photographs: J. Allan Cash 8, 10, 15, 28; Heather Angel 26; ZEFA 13,
14, 21, 24, 25, 29.

Printed in the United States of America

1 2 3 4 5 6 7 8 9 99 98 97 96 95

Hearing

By Henry Pluckrose
Photographs by Chris Fairclough

Gareth Stevens Publishing
MILWAUKEE

Sit very still indoors.
Try not to move.

4

Listen very carefully. What sounds can you hear?

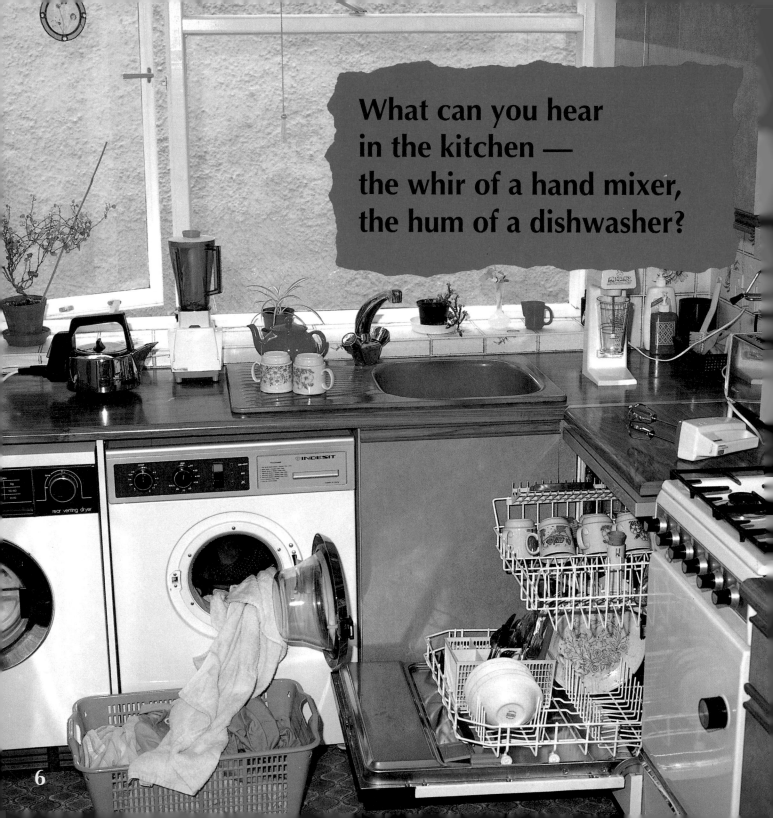

What can you hear
in the kitchen —
the whir of a hand mixer,
the hum of a dishwasher?

6

Listen to sounds outside. Can you hear the distant roar of traffic or the rumble of a train?

7

Sounds are louder when
you are near them.
What sound does a train make
rushing on the tracks?

This jet plane has just taken off.
Its engines roar loudly.

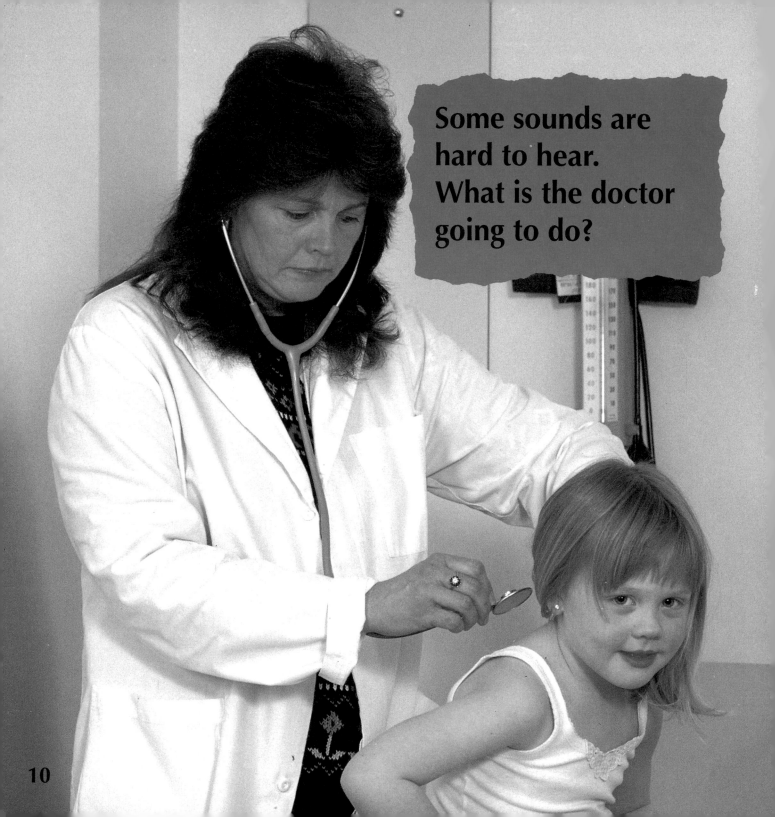

Some sounds are hard to hear. What is the doctor going to do?

10

This man is printing newspapers.
Why is he wearing earmuffs?

11

Some sounds are sharp and sudden. A balloon bursts with a pop.

12

Some sounds seem to go on forever. The chatter of people in a busy market never stops.

13

Some loud sounds
warn of danger.
What noise does
a fire engine make
when it's in a hurry?

14

Have you ever heard
bells chiming?
Why do people
ring bells?

Imagine that you are taking the
next few pictures in this book.
What sounds do you hear?

16

17

Sounds are everywhere —
the pitter-patter of rain . . .

the thundering crash of
waves against rocks . . .

23

the crow of
a rooster . . .

the grunts
of pigs . . .

25

the buzz of
a bee . . .

the purr
of a cat.

Some sounds are
soft and gentle.

28

Others are loud and sometimes frightening.

Some sounds are so faint
you can hardly hear them.

Sit very still outside and
listen carefully.
What sounds can you hear?

More Books to Read

Ears Are for Hearing. Paul Showers (Crowell)
Hearing. Kathie B. Smith (Troll)
Listen . . .What Do You Hear? J. Rye and N. Wood (Troll)

Videotapes

Clifford's Fun with Sounds. (Scholastic)
Sound. (Coronet/MTI Film and Video)
Use Your Ears. (Barr Films)

Activities for Learning and Fun

1. Eco-Sounds Listen to tapes that have a variety of sounds from nature. Can you identify all the animals and other outdoor noises you hear on the tape? Use a tape recorder to make your own tape of sounds in nature. See if family members or friends can identify the sounds you have recorded.

2. Hear! Hear! Listen to the different levels of sounds, or pitches, that can be made using a variety of rubber bands. Stretch the rubber bands over or around bowls, pans, jars, vases, or other open containers. Pluck the stretched rubber bands with your finger, as if you are playing a guitar. Do some of the rubber bands make sounds that are higher than others? Lower? How many different pitches can you hear?

Index